Love to Shelley
    From Cousin Myrtle
        Dec. 1984

**Candles in the Dark**

Trust this tree story
Will be a real
blessing to you —
    Col. 3rd Chapter

Christmas Blessing
Myrtle
"1962"

"from
The Gillette"
Stonecroft

# Candles in the Dark

*Letters of Amy Carmichael*

A DOHNAVUR BOOK

**CHRISTIAN LITERATURE CRUSADE**
Fort Washington, Pennsylvania 19034

First published 1981
Triangle
SPCK
Holy Trinity Church
Marylebone Road
London NW1 4DU

All rights reserved. No part of this book may be
reproduced or transmitted in any form or by any means,
electronic or mechanical, including photocopying,
recording, or by an information storage and retrieval
system without permission in writing from the publisher.

Copyright The Dohnavur Fellowship 1981

First American Edition 1982

ISBN 87508-085-5

Christian Literature Crusade
Fort Washington, Pennsylvania 19034

**DOHNAVUR BOOKS**
**by Amy Carmichael**
Published by SPCK

**Stories of Indian Women**
Mimosa (paper)

**Devotional Books**
His Thoughts Said . . . His Father Said . . . (paper)
Edges of His Ways (paper)
If (paper)
God's Missionary (paper)
Gold by Moonlight (cased)

**Verse**
Towards Jerusalem (paper)

**BIOGRAPHY**
Amy Carmichael of Dohnavur (paper)
BY FRANK HOUGHTON

# Contents

# Introduction

Amy Carmichael was born in Northern Ireland and after a brief period in Japan arrived in India on 9 November 1895 as a Keswick missionary. She never left India till her death in Dohnavur on 18 January 1951. At first she worked in the villages of South India. Then in 1901 she began to make a home for children in need of protection and care. Others came to help her and the Dohnavur Fellowship was born—named after the village in which it is situated. For fifty years she was Mother ('Amma') to an ever-increasing family and saw many of her children grow up to serve the Lord by serving others.

In 1931 an accident led to illness and increasing physical limitations. For the last years of her life she was confined to bed, but her indomitable spirit never failed. She continued to counsel and encourage all who came to see her and wrote many books and innumerable letters.

The following letters, written with no thought of publication, have been selected from many hundreds treasured by members of the Dohnavur Fellowship, either her colleagues or her Indian children. Her power to help those in need came from her times of listening to her Lord. 'Sometimes,' she wrote, 'it is as if another Hand were turning over the pages of my Bible and finding the places for me.' Her language is steeped in the older versions of the Bible (she died before many of the modern translations appeared), and a lifetime spent in India gave her an Indian mode of thought.

'Pray for me, that the Lord would give me house room again to hold a candle to this dark world', wrote Samuel

Rutherford, and this was Amy's prayer. It is our prayer too, as we share the riches she passed on to us through her close personal walk with the Lord and utter devotion to Him.

B. M. G. TREHANE
Dohnavur Fellowship

# 1 Discipleship

God needs those
who are ready to lay down
their very lives
to lead others into true soldiership
and a true following of
the Crucified.

# Training for service

The best training is to learn to accept everything as it comes, as from Him whom our soul loves. The tests are always unexpected things, not great things that can be written up, but the common little rubs of life, silly little nothings, things you are ashamed of minding one scrap. Yet they can knock a strong man over and lay him very low.

It is a very good thing to learn to take things by the right handle. An inward grouse is a devastating thing. I expect you know this, we all do; but it is extraordinary how the devil tries to 'get' us on the ordinary road of life. But all is well if only we are in Him, deep in Him, and He in us our daily strength and joy and song.

I have read and re-read the bit in your letter about the love that constrains. Nothing less will hold on to the end. Feelings can be shaken and the fight can be fearfully discouraging, for sometimes we seem to be losing ground and all seems to be going wrong. Then the devil comes and paints glorious pictures of what might have been. He did to me—I can see those pictures still. But as we go on steadfastly obeying the word that compelled, we do become aware that it is all worthwhile. We *know* it, we *know* Him with us, and that is life.

I am going to ask that the consciousness of His presence with you may be constant and very sweet. I know the difference this makes. But you are not a child in Him; you have passed the point where that is needful. You *know* Him near, with you and in you. Joy though it be to be conscious of that blessed One, the great thing is not my feeling, but His fact. So if there are fogs on the sea on any day or any night—still all's well.

## Soldiers

It matters a good deal that your book-food should be strong meat. We are what we think about. Think about trivial things or weak things and somehow one loses fibre and becomes flabby in spirit. Soldiers need to be strong.

Soldiers have not time for everything. 'I have no time for anything outside my profession,' a young officer said once, and in measure that is true. We can't be entangled in the affairs of this life if we are to be real soldiers. By its affairs I mean its chatter and its ways of thinking and deciding questions, its whole aspect and trend.

## *Everything matters*

My prayer for each of you is that you labour in the work from the rising of the morning till the stars appear (Nehemiah 4.21): that is, from your earliest days, the days of your morning, till the last days, the days of your evening, when He whom not seeing you love will call you home to see His face.

Some of you, who are longing to live this life, still hesitate. There is no life in all the world so joyful. It has pain in it, too, but looking back I can tell you truly, there is far more joy than pain. Do not hesitate. Give yourselves wholly to your Lord to be prepared for whatever He has chosen for you to do.

Many of you *are* preparing for service. This is my word for you: Don't say 'It doesn't matter' about anything (except your own feelings), for everything matters. Everything is important, even the tiniest thing. If you do everything, whether great or small, for the sake of your Saviour and Lord, then you will be ready for whatever work He has chosen for you to do later.

## A new fellowship

Sooner or later I do trust that your best loved ones will understand and be in sympathy. It must have seemed strange to the angels when our Lord Jesus emptied Himself and came to earth, to live a poor man's life and die a felon's death. It must have hurt them too. I know this must have been a holy pain, but even so I think it could not have been easy for our Lord to let them suffer at all. And what of the Father's suffering? The only beloved Son could not lightly see His Father suffer as He gave Him up for us all. So He, Jesus your Lord, can enter into even this with you, and He does. And if He calls you into a new fellowship with Him in His suffering I know that you will not draw back.

'Across the will of nature
    Leads on the path of God;
Not where the flesh delighteth
    The feet of Jesus trod.'

'Oh Jesus, Thy care is not to make
    The desert a waste no more,
But to keep our feet lest we miss the track
    Where Thy feet went before.'

## Facing new work

One morning I woke with these words on my lips: 'We follow a stripped and crucified Saviour.' Those words go very deep. They touch everything, one's outer life as well as one's inner; motives, purposes, decisions, everything. Let them be with you as you prepare for the new life. It is sure to have tests, unexpected tests as well as many an unexpected joy. But if you follow a stripped and crucified Saviour, and by the power of His resurrection seek to enter into the fellowship of His sufferings, you will go on in peace and be one of those blessed ones who spread peace all round.

> Deep in me, Lord, mark Thou Thy holy cross,
>     On motives, choices, private dear desires;
> Let all that self in any form inspires
>     Be unto me as dross.
>
> And when Thy touch of death is here and there
>     Laid on a thing most precious in my eyes,
> Let me not wonder, let me recognize
>     The answer to my prayer.

## *To a young worker*

The fight to which we have been called is not an easy fight.
We are touching the very centre of the devil's power and
kingdom, and he hates us intensely and fights hard against
us. We have no chance at all of winning in this fight unless
we are disciplined soldiers, utterly out-and-out and
uncompromising, and men and women of prayer.

So first, give much time to quietness. We have to get our
help for the most part direct from our God. We are here to
help, not to be helped, and we must each one of us learn to
walk with God alone and feed on His word so as to be
nourished. Don't only read and pray; *listen*. And don't
evade the slightest whisper of guidance that comes. God
make you very sensitive, and very obedient.

Fill up the crevices of time with the things that matter
most. This will cost something, but it is worth it. 'Seek ye
My face. My heart said unto Thee, Thy face, Lord, will I
seek.' No one is of much use who does not truly want to
learn what it means to pray and listen and definitely choose
the life that is hid with Christ in God.

Keep close, keep close. If you are close you will be keen.
Your heart will be set on the things that abide. You will
drink of His spirit and you will thirst for souls even as He
thirsts. You will not be attracted by the world that
crucified Him, but you will love the people in that world
who have never seen His beauty and are losing so much
more than they know. You will live to share your joy in
Him. Nothing else will count for much.

All this will be, if you walk with Him as with a visible
Companion, from dawn through all the hours till you go to
sleep at night. And your nights may be holy too, every
waking moment a loving turning to Him who is watching
over your sleep as your Mother watched over it when you
were a tiny child.

Your dear ones: commit them to Him. It is the Wounded
Hands that part you. That was said to me when the

7

stabbing pain of the parting was almost too much to bear. It was the thought of their pain that broke me; it may be like that with you. Then take the word that comforted me: it is the Wounded Hands that part you, one on them, the other on you, and He will not leave them comfortless. It is hard to say goodbyes, like being torn in pieces without chloroform. But it is for His sake; that carries one through.

## To one who had slipped

I am quite sure that 'the angel's slackened hand' allowed that slip to be because of the immense help it would be later on. This sounds illogical, but Love has amazing ways of leading us to the place where we can help most.

The one person who stands out in my memory as one incapable of ever helping others was one who never suffered—never even had a headache. She had beautiful children, but apparently never even suffered then. She was incapable of understanding pain in others.

I have often thought of her and been thankful for pain. In a similar way, though of course different, a slip on the upward climb is sometimes the one way by which we can be led into Hebrews 5.2.* For if one doesn't know by startling experience the peril of such things—such subtle things—one might not be able to enter into the experience with others. And we would not be quick and aware to come to the rescue *before* the wolf has leaped.

*Hebrews 5.2: . . . who can bear gently with the ignorant and erring, for that He Himself also is compassed with infirmity (RV).

9

## Damascus steel

I care much more that you should be what God means you to be than that you should always be pleased with what I say. One thing I promise you. I will say 'to' you, not 'of'.

You want to be Damascus steel, not soft iron. So I think you will find that those who care most do sometimes act as cold water (the great Forger of sword blades does the fire and hammer part), but it is because they see something that can be turned to steel. Isn't that a comfort?

## Forgiven

This word often comes to me: 'Forgiven – from Egypt
even until now.' God has forgiven me far more than I have
ever forgiven you, so you see it is as one who has been
forgiven much that I forgive you—not as one who never
needs forgiveness. We love because He forgives. You
remember our Lord's question about that (Luke 7.42).
Oh, let us more and more deeply love the Forgiving
Saviour and more and more walk softly with Him lest we
grieve Him in any tiny thing. That is what I want to do,
and I know you do too.

Now all is forgotten, buried in the sea. I will never think
of it again. It is *gone*.

## To one depressed by failure

1 John 1.9 is my word too. 'If we confess our sins, He is faithful and righteous to forgive us our sins, and to cleanse us from all unrighteousness.'

There is more in me to be forgiven than in any of you. I think I must be rather like the woman who loved much because she was forgiven much.

The Lord has borne with me all these years. How *can* He? Oh, His patience, His continuance in love, knowing all and yet still loving—it is too wonderful for me ever to understand. He takes the dust we lay at the foot of the cross.

Isn't this a nice version of Isaiah 46.4: 'I have made and I will put up with thee.' It has been my word lately—so comforting—and I give it to you.

## Pour out all

A word in Deuteronomy that brought you to me when I read it some days ago is this: 'The Lord is their Inheritance as He hath said unto them' (Deuteronomy 18.2). I thought then, as I think now, of the lovely inheritance you might have had. But He is your Inheritance instead of that lovely earthly joy. Throughout all eternity that word will be opening up its treasures.

You will never regret your choice. It is wonderful to be free to pour out all, every drop of one's life; and that is what you have done and are doing. No, you will never regret it, never.

## To one who felt useless

My first feeling was to write and tell you that you are mistaken, but though I think you are, in part, I won't write so. Instead, I will say what our heavenly Father said to me long ago, and says to me still very often: 'See in it a chance to die.'

Perhaps the brave love of God is touching with death the *I* in you, that it may be in very truth 'not I but Christ'. This is your heart's desire, your deepest desire, and He counts nothing too much to do, that it may be fully fulfilled. 'Ponder the voice of my humble desire.' He has pondered it; He is answering it. So be of good cheer. Don't heed the devil's whisper about uselessness. Is he not the father of lies? Why believe a liar? God is working out a most beautiful purpose.

Now good night, and let the Lord give His beloved sleep untroubled by the unkind remarks of the enemy. Believe me, he is not at all trustworthy, and you well know your Lord is. Does He *ever* break His word? No, never, and He knows that you know it. 'For Thou, Lord, hast never failed them that fear Thee.' No, nor ever will.

# Live in Romans 8

I think often we miss much by not being simple enough. Don't you think so? The little-child confidence is what He wants. It is true we are nothing, just nothing, but then He doesn't love us because we are something. He has called you. Of that I have not one atom of doubt, and whom He calls He justifies. (As you quote that word, I do too.) 'And whom He justified, them He also glorified.' And go on, it is simply wonderful. 'What shall we say then to these things? If God be for us, who can be against us?' Not even our own selves, our *I* that we feel is so distressingly against all we long to be. Live in Romans 8 and let the rest go by. That is your abiding place, not Romans 7.

As I thought of you early this morning, this came:

> Thou hast called me—I cannot tell why.
> Thou wilt justify me—I cannot tell how.
> Thou wilt glorify me—I cannot tell when.

It is all too wonderful for me when I think of myself, not you. I can believe it for you. But can it be true for me? Yes, it must be true, because He has said it.

## *To one afraid of failing*

It is those who never fear a fall who fall most terribly.
'Hold thou me up and I shall be safe'; not for one moment
is our own power enough.

I think our Lord demands all. I see nothing less in His
.words about taking up the cross. It is all or nothing. I
don't mean that one sees all there is to see at first, or even
at last, but only that all we know is given because we want
to give all.

> And faith shall sing a joyous Yes
> To every dear command of Thine.

He poured out all for us. Can we measure our offering to
Him?

Don't be anxious. It is not what we feel that is
important. By His grace, who has grace sufficient for the
weakest of us, do you will to do His will? Do you will to
do it even if it brings sorrow and pain and weariness? Yes,
and dullness? If you can say, 'He enabling me, that is my
desire', then you need not fear. You will not fail.

## Loneliness

On this day many years ago I went away alone to a cave in a mountain called Arima, in Japan. I felt many feelings of fear about the future. That was why I went there. I wanted to be alone with God.

The devil kept on whispering, 'It's all right now, but what about afterwards? You are going to be very lonely.' And he painted pictures of loneliness. I can see them still. Then I turned to my God in a kind of desperation and said, 'Lord, what can I do? How can I go on to the end?' And He said, 'None of them that trust in Me shall be desolate' (Psalm 34.22).

That word has been with me ever since, and I give it to you now. It has been fulfilled to me. It will be fulfilled to you. Only live for Him who redeemed you and trust Him to take care of you, *and He will*.

That day the words 'not only but also' were given to me too. There is not only joy but also sorrow in every life, but in the end—O in the end we shall see His face and we shall serve Him together.

## To a future leader

I give you as a precious jewel a word from *Colossian Studies* which came to me afresh this morning. It is Bishop Moule's rendering of 'Unto all pleasing' (chapter 1.10). '*To all meeting of His wishes*—so as not only to obey explicit precepts but as it were to anticipate in everything His "sweet, beloved will" always, everywhere.' This is life. No other life is worth living. The Lord make it true of your life and of mine.

Looking ahead, if He tarry, I can see for you attack of many kinds, painful days, travail. But this I know: you will regret nothing when you look back, except lack of faith or fortitude or love. You will never regret having thrown all to the winds in order to follow your Master and Lord. Nothing will seem too much to have done or suffered, when, in the end, we see Him and the marks of His wounds; nothing will ever seem enough. Even the weariness of deferred hope will be forgotten, in the joy that is not of earth. And even now the overweights of joy are often more than we had asked or thought.

I shall not fear difficulties for you, for I know 'it is the very work of grace to transform difficulties into opportunities'—a word from Paget's *The Spirit of Discipline* which I have proved true. But I shall ask that the greater the difficulty, the more abundant the supply of love may be, so that you will love your way through all and prove the conquering power of love—eternal love.

## Unity

I depend on you to carry on whatever happens. There may be difficult days ahead, but if you all stand together and go on together, nothing can overwhelm you. There may be attacks upon the pattern shown, and upon your vital unity which is founded upon loyal love. Be it so. I cannot fear. He who has called will hold you fast, and He will lead you on.

But it will need care. 'Look, therefore, *carefully* how you walk', as Westcott translates Ephesians 5.15. Anything so attacked as loyal unity is attacked does need care if it is to be preserved. We need to walk humbly not only with our God but with one another, lest the enemy slip in at some unguarded gateway and poison the sweetness of our life together. In this as in all I count on you to help.

# 'While'

You are His very much trusted one. When the day comes that sees you facing the sword, not peace, for someone you have led to the Lord, you will understand why this experience of the sword has been allowed—no, has *had* to be. I shall never forget my first deep heart-rending time with a child in the Faith. I knew then why my own heart had to be rent.

But I thank Him for the comfort. 'For our light affliction, which is but for a moment, worketh for us a far more exceeding and eternal weight of glory; *while* we look not at the things which are seen, but at the things which are not seen: for the things which are seen are temporal; but the things which are not seen are eternal' (2 Corinthians 4.17, 18).

## *To the uncommitted*

A few evenings ago I was reading about our Lord Jesus in
the high priest's house, where He was so cruelly handled
that one can hardly bear to think of more pain for Him.
And then came poor Peter's denial, and He heard that
denial. It must have been a thousand times more hurting
than any other thing that night. 'And the Lord turned and
looked on Peter.' Soon afterwards those loving eyes were
blindfolded.

I thought, 'If in a few minutes my eyes were to be
blindfolded, how should I wish to use them before that was
done?' And I remembered some of you who are wandering
further from Him than Peter wandered. Oh to be able to
turn and look on them! But I cannot. They are not in the
room with me. And then I remembered, *He can; He does.*
Even now, as my heart longs over them, His heart is
longing with a far greater longing. And in His eyes is
something that can never be in mine: *power to convict, to
recall.*

Think of those eyes that were blindfolded. Put your
name where I leave a blank space: 'And the Lord turned
and looked upon —————.' May the next words be
true of you: 'And ————— went out and wept
bitterly.'

## 2 Life and Work

Think of yourself
as belonging first to your Lord
and then to all, Servant of all.
In serving any one of the 'all'
you are serving Him who is your Lord.
Life is never lonely or empty
if we keep Him where He must always be,
in the first place.

## One thing I do

I often think how wonderful it is to have nothing to think of, no care in all the world but to do His will and finish His work. There are sorrows—there must be in a world so full of sorrow—but 'This one thing I do' can be our word. And there is joy in that.

I have been reading Ephesians 3.10, 11. 'The Powers in the heavenly places' are real powers. If only we by the grace of God live lives that glorify our Lord, if only we are not overcome by griefs and trials such as those we are passing through now, but look above them and go on in peace, then something of the wonderful wisdom of God will be shown to those Unseen Watchers. It is a solemn thought, for of course the opposite is true. If we are 'overcome of evil' we show nothing of His love and grace and all that is meant by His 'manifold wisdom'. Oh, may He help us not to lose this opportunity to glorify His Name.

# Caring for children

The salvation of a single child—who can measure what that may mean not only here but There? You can't do everything. 'After it, follow it, follow the Gleam.' For us the Gleam is the salvation of children, and it involves the prosaic towel. 'He took a towel.' So we won't mind if our feet are bound, for it is Love that binds them.* His were bound on the cross.

* Tamil proverb: 'Children bind the mother's feet.'

## To a young mother

This morning I was reading in Luke, and as I read of the angels' joy over the birth of our Saviour and thought of their joy over everyone born again into the Kingdom, I felt sure they rejoice over every precious little life born into a family of true lovers of our Lord. And I thought how to each little one an angel is given. How little we know of these heavenly things, but I do like to think of the angel prepared for your little treasure and, above all, to think of what has been prepared for that little one 'before the foundation of the world'. How much more there is in a baby than just sweetness and the appealing innocence of baby days. All the great thoughts of God lie behind that little life, all the great purposes. Ephesians chapters 1 and 2 tell of these. The more one ponders, the more one wonders.

## A double yoke

I am thinking so much of you. My prayer for you is that the peace of God may enter into your heart so that you will spread peace all round.

The only way I know that leads to this is the way of Matthew 11.29. Verse 28 has a word for you, too, but verse 29 is all for you. You have borne a yoke—sometimes a heavy yoke—but *His* yoke is easy and His burden is light, because we do not bear it alone. *It is a double yoke.* We are fellow-workers with Him in a new sense, when we give up making our own yoke and take His. It is a definite transaction between Him and our souls. *'Take.'* He won't put it on us; He asks us to take. Then when we do, it is His yoke, not ours, thereafter.

## *Go ye*

The glorious word of the Lord stands sure. He said, 'Go ye'. You have gone. He said, 'You shall be witnesses'. You are His witness. He said, 'I am with you all the days'. He is with you now. And He has said that your labour shall *not* be in vain. So it will not be in vain.

When the enemy comes like a storm against a wall let the Spirit of the Lord lift up like a standard in your heart these great eternal truths. They will not fail you; He will not fail you, and He will watch over His seed.

## *I have nothing*

I have been thinking of you as you begin work today. The story of the man who said, 'I have nothing to set before him', has been helping me this morning (not for the first time). It says so exactly what I so often feel. 'A friend of mine in his journey has come to me and I have nothing to set before him'—no, not even a crumb.

I expect you also often feel like that. I can well understand how the devil will make you feel like that poor man who had nothing to give and went in the night to borrow three loaves. But the end of the story is very comforting, 'He will rise and give him as many as he needs.' As much as you need to do His will and help others, these travellers in life's difficult journey, will be given to you to give. There will be no shortage from the heavenly point of view. So meet the devil's depressing whisper, as I pray this morning that I may, with that dear word, 'as many as he needs', and be at peace.

## God's morrow

This morning as I listened God's word to me was in Acts 10—something I had never noticed before: Peter must have wanted to get quickly to those waiting souls, he must have seen them in imagination, and he was always of an eager spirit—not phlegmatic. And yet he waited, and 'on the morrow he arose'. God give me this quietness, the quietness that can wait as I think of needy bodies, and souls too, and many other things. God's morrow—I don't want to hurry that morrow.

Isn't the Bible amazing? 'In Scripture every little daisy is a meadow.' Blessed be God for our meadow.

## A pure work

Don't be surprised if there is attack on your work, on *you* who are called to do it, on your innermost nature—the hidden man of the heart. It must be so. The great thing is not to be surprised, not to count it strange—for that plays into the hand of the enemy.

Is it possible that anyone should set himself to exalt our beloved Lord and *not* become instantly a target for many arrows? The very fact that your work depends utterly on Him and can't be done for a moment without Him calls for a very close walk and a constant communion of spirit. This alone is enough to account for anything the enemy can do.

But there are limits set. Greater is He. I have just read that glorious word in Romans 5, 'They that receive the abundance of grace . . . reign in life, through the One, even Jesus Christ.' And this was written to slaves in Nero's wicked palace. What daring of faith the Spirit gave to Paul.

It *costs* to have a pure work. Not for nothing is our God called a Consuming Fire.

## Not weaklings but warriors

'He [Moses] endured as seeing Him who is invisible.' You cannot see the loving eyes of your Lord or see His hand stretched out to help you. And yet you are trusted to go on *just as if you saw*. You are trusted to endure as seeing Him who is invisible, your Redeemer, your Captain and your Lord.

There is no life that is not at times hardly beset. We are not called to be weaklings but warriors. So let no one be surprised when the enemy comes in like a flood. But there is no need ever to be overwhelmed. There is not one word in the Bible to tell us to expect to be overwhelmed, for the moment the enemy comes like a flood, that very moment the Spirit of the Lord lifts up a standard against him (Isaiah 59.19) and makes us strong to endure as seeing Him who is invisible.

## 'I know thy . . . ministry'

You know Campbell Morgan's thought about ministry being different from works. He sees it as the unofficial, untabulated little loving kindnesses of life. I looked the word up in Young's Concordance. It's the word used of Martha preparing food for our Lord Jesus, such an ordinary, everyday sort of thing, nothing she would expect to be remembered.

He remembers every single little inconspicuous thing—quite apart from the big things, the 'works'. What a loving memory He has.

## An unfathomable jewel mine

The message for tomorrow evening is rich. You will give it as something that has helped *you*, won't you? Otherwise it is just an interesting little Bible study. The great thing is to give what has strengthened and kindled your own soul. Then it is sure to kindle others.

I think many will be brought to the place where they are ready not only for light about problems, but also for a new revelation of the Purpose and Counsel of God for each one individually and for all as a part of the Household of God.

It is an unfathomable jewel mine—this Book of ours. I have large expectations. 'Lord, all my desires are before Thee.'

## *Our priestly garments*

Did you know that the high priest in olden days was just an ordinary man except when he wore his priestly garments? I had thought of Aaron as walking about in some of them, at least, much as a clergyman wears his dog collar. But it wasn't so.

Our Lord, the beauty of our Lord and His Righteousness—these are our priestly garments. Without that clothing we have no priestly rights, powers or virtues whatsoever. It is just another illustration of 'Without Me ye can do nothing', *be* nothing too.

## Hidden purposes

Our God *does* satisfy. I think sometimes He has to draw us into strange experiences in order that we shall prove Him to the uttermost, for some purpose out of sight.

For what is He preparing us? It is all hidden, we have only hints in the Gospels and in Revelation. 'His servants shall serve Him'—where? how? But this we do know: never a pang of disappointment or loneliness or pain (there are many different kinds of pangs) but may be turned to minister towards a perfecting of power to serve—first here on earth, then Otherwhere.

## Filling gaps

If only X could see that filling up gaps is a really full-time work often, and just invaluable, it would help. But did you ever know a *young* Christian worker who could understand that? Of the dozens I have had to do with I can't remember one who saw that truth under ten years! It's a very mature sort of truth.

## Peace for others

You have been brought through a very busy time in peace. If peace be not broken, all is well. I was thinking today of the words in Luke 8.46, 48. Power went forth from our Lord; it cost Him something to heal. And that power which went forth from Him passed into the poor sick woman and in her it became peace. 'Go in peace', He said to her. So as you pour forth power to help others, that power—if you are living deep in your Lord and Master and drinking deep of His Spirit—will pass into peace for others; help and healing and peace.

## The individual touch

Yesterday I read and read Luke 4.40. It was as if I had never seen it before. Those crowds—hot, sticky, clamorous, tiresome probably; but He did not see them as crowds. He laid His hands on every one of them—*every one of them*.

It's the individual touch that tells. He doesn't love in the mass, but in ones. 'Not a sparrow . . .'

## For a new year

This last year has been a year of battle, but thank God of victory too, and we are nearer the Crowning Day this morning than ever we were before. 'And having done all to stand.' God keep us standing. 'When I said, My foot slippeth, Thy mercy, O Lord, held me up.'

And now as we look forward we see great stones and many of them. 'Who shall roll away the stone?' More and more I delight in the word that says, 'The angel of the Lord descended from heaven and came and rolled back the stone *and sat upon it*.' We shall see the angel of the Lord sitting upon many a stone during the coming year. And think of it, we may see the Lord Himself, Christ risen, Christ crowned, *this year*. Oh what will it be to see Him? To be for ever with Him, holy for ever, strong for ever, never, never to grieve Him again.

# The wind of the Spirit

How I rejoice. Yes, now your boat will go out to sea in a new way. We have not to make the Wind or to beseech it to blow. We have nothing to do with the wonder of it. Our one work is to set our sails to catch the least whisper of it. 'Blow, blow O Breath' really only means, 'O Breath, my sails are set; according to the promise of my Lord, fill them now.'

And what is it to Him if the boat be small or great? All the wind asks for is a sail set to catch that which is ready to fill the merest nothing of us all.

The one condition for receiving is obedience; and the one condition for going on is the same. Yield to the impulse to pray, to sing, to speak, to be silent—to be or to do anything. Never stifle the Spirit. Never grieve Him by arguing or disregarding. Quench not the Spirit, vex not the Spirit. All the verbs are gentle. It is as if our God would have us understand that the blessed filling of the Blessed Spirit is a very tender thing, that *He* is very tender. A very slight dimness on the glass obscures the image. A very little rust on the blade mars its perfection. So with all sensitive things. So with Him and His power to effect through us what He will. If we disregard some quiet inward admonition, then suddenly or gradually (but surely) our sail starts flapping against the mast. We make no headway, and we seek for Him, but there is a sense of absence. And that is pain to the loving heart.

But if ever this should be, go back to where you were when you first set your sail. 'To them that obey Him.' Then, oh so quickly, so gladly, the blessed Wind will blow again. He never keeps us waiting, unless indeed we have kept Him long waiting, and then sometimes, as in the Song of Songs (chapter 5, the third wandering), there is a pause between missing Him and welcoming Him again.

But may such an experience never be yours. It need never, never be.

## Freed from graveclothes

Recently the devil made a dead set at our prayer life; it froze. I was miserable about it and at last told how I felt we should *perish* if we were not revived. And all responded, and the daily prayer meetings became what they never should have ceased to be; vital. Then to one and another a hunger was given, and now they have received such an overflowing joy in God that they 'cannot but speak'.

It is wonderful. The attitude of many is so changed towards things in general—difficulties for example—that I can hardly thank God enough.

I have been feeling for months that God is waiting to show what He can do through a company of people wholly at His service, freed from graveclothes, at liberty. Oh that not one may hang back!

God is still working. But why do I say 'still', as if I expected Him to stop working for a while? Indeed I do not!

# Guidance

I think that in guidance God deals with us as He dealt with the Israelites. The first crossing of the sea was made very easy, the guidance could not have been simpler. The strong east wind blew and divided the sea before the people had to cross; not a foot was wet, except perhaps by the driving spray.

But how different it was on the second occasion, when God taught them to obey without, as it were, making it first of all impossible to disobey. The priests had to stand still in the water of the river. What a sight for men to scoff at, that standing still in the water! But it was not till they obeyed, and without a particle of visible proof that they were doing right, went on to carry the ark right into the river, that the water rolled back before them.

So, it seems to me, we may as we go on with God be called again and again to go right into our rivers, to wet our feet in them. We may be called to do what nobody understands but those to whom the word has come and the promise. But the word *must* come first and the promise too. We must be sure, with an inward conviction that absolutely *nothing* can shake.

In my own case again and again I have had to wet my feet in the water. But when the Red Sea kind of guidance is given I am always very glad, for then others can see, and that does help. You know those lines in Hannington's *Life*;

> He saw a hand they could not see
> That beckoned him away,
> He heard a voice they could not hear
> That would not let him stay.

Only God and those who have to walk in that path know how hard it can be. But He does know, and when the people about us don't hear the words of the voice, but only say 'It thunders', well, He comes near, and we know Him as we never knew Him before. At least so it seems to me.

## Wetted feet

I am not sure that I would feel guidance lay in all doors shutting behind. I have never yet moved on without several doors being wide open behind and many hands pushing me in through one or other of those doors. I think the picture of the unwetted feet in the first crossing over water, and the wetted feet in the second, when a lesson of guidance far deeper than the first had to be given, is full of teaching for us. What I would think much more of is that inward urge; and as for outward things, well, no need to speak of them. To the watching eye and the listening ear they are clear enough. And then with that usually comes a loving word of peace.

But for the present there is just one thing to be done. Never let a possible tomorrow muddle up today, or shadow it, or confuse it. Nothing that comes in the day's work is waste; it will all fit in one day.

## The next step

If the next step is clear, then the one thing to do is to take it. Don't pledge your Lord or yourself about the steps beyond. You don't see them yet.

Once when I was climbing at night in the forest before there was a made path, I learned what the word meant, Psalm 119.105: 'Thy word is a *lantern* to my path'. I had a lantern and had to hold it very low or I should certainly have slipped on those rough rocks. We don't walk spiritually by electric light but by a hand lantern. And a lantern only shows the next step—not several ahead.

## Knowing God's will

'May Thy grace, O Lord, make that possible to me which seems impossible to me by nature.'

'Blessed are the single-hearted, for they shall enjoy much peace.'

There can be only one right way, one right thing to say or do. If you refuse to be hurried and pressed, if you stay your soul on God, nothing can keep you from that clearness of spirit which is life and peace. In that stillness you will know what His will is. Strength and calm will come to do it. You will go on with Him, and you will prove Him in new ways and grow in strength and joy.

## Anywhere, Lord

Don't be surprised if temptations come. The one way is to throw yourself, everything you have to give, into the service to which you have been called. Paul spoke of himself as an offering poured out on 'the sacrifice and service of your faith' (Philippians 2.17). That's what you must be, nothing kept back. And as you give all, you find all.

Often His call is to follow in paths we would not have chosen. But if in truth we say, 'Anywhere, Lord', He takes us at our word and orders our goings, and then He puts a new song in our mouths, even a thanksgiving unto our God (Psalm 40 verses 2, 3 Prayer Book Version). There is wonderful joy to be had from knowing that we are *not* in the way of our own choice. At least I have found it so. It gives a peculiar sort of confidence that even we—we who are nothings—are being 'ordered' in our goings. It is very good to be 'ordered' by our beloved Lord.

## To one facing an 'impossible' task

I woke between one and two o'clock and prayed oh such poor prayers for you. I was troubled about their poorness till I suddenly remembered in whose Name I prayed. That was enough. The Father so loves His beloved Son that the poorest little word that rises in His name touches His heart. So you woke into a prayer.

Go with an open mind to be led at the time—not with all arranged beforehand. It is great to be faced with the impossible, for nothing is impossible if one is meant to do it. Wisdom will be given, and strength. When the Lord leads He *always* strengthens.

# 'All' means 'all'

'All the paths of the Lord are lovingkindness.' I found that in RV lately (Psalm 25.10) and have found it feeds. *All* does not mean 'all but these paths we are in now' or 'nearly all, but perhaps not just this specially difficult painful one'. All must mean *all*. So your path with its unexplained sorrow, and mine with its unexplained sharp flints and briers, and both with their unexplained perplexity of guidance, their sheer mystery, are just lovingkindness, nothing less. I am resting my heart on that word. It bears one up on eagle's wings; it gives courage and song and sweetness too, that sweetness of spirit which it is death to lose even for one half hour.

God bless you and utterly satisfy your heart with Himself. I remember in old days almost desperately repeating to myself these lines from Tersteegen:

> Am I not enough, Mine own?
>   Enough Mine own for thee? . . .
> Am I not enough Mine own?
>   I for ever and alone,
>     *I*, needing *thee*?

It was a long time before I could say honestly 'Yes' to that question. I remember the turmoil of soul as if it were yesterday, but at last, oh the rest, 'for in acceptance lieth peace'.

## His way is perfect

Did you know that the word translated 'determinate' in Acts 2.23 is the word from which our word 'horizon' is derived? That opens thoughts, doesn't it? Nothing happened to our Lord Jesus that did not come within the boundaries of the Father's purposes. And as Ephesians teaches us, our lives are planned in the same way.

It doesn't much matter what happens to us. The one thing that matters is how we meet what happens. Limitations, frustrations—they can't cast the smallest handful of dust on the glory of God. So let us be of good courage. He is leading us through and on, and as for God, His way is perfect.

# Today

'The Lamb which is in the midst of the throne . . . shall lead them unto living fountains of water' Revelation 7.17. We shall be led to living fountains of water There, the head waters, high up on the mountain, and we shall drink and be for ever satisfied. But what about today?

We drink of the brook in the way today, the torrent, the very same water as that of which we shall drink afterwards when the mountain is climbed. (You know Kay on Psalm 110.7: 'He shall drink on his way of the torrent.') I never put the two thoughts together before. The living fountain of waters tomorrow, those same waters flowing downhill for us in the brook by the way—*today*.

# 3 Pain and Suffering

CHRIST suffered in the flesh.
If those who follow Him in obedience now
are called to suffer (as they will be),
they can conquer if they 'arm themselves
with the same mind' (1 Peter 4.1).
He looked on to the glory which should follow.
So they.

## Prayer for healing

Your prayer for perfect healing went to my heart. God knows how I long to be well and able to do more. But yesterday as I read Psalm 84.11, 'No good thing will He withhold from them that live a godly life', I wondered if He would not rather the emphasis were laid on this: 'Draw us so into accord with Thyself that no good thing shall be withheld', instead of: 'Health is a good thing. Lord, give it.'

More than three times I have prayed Paul's prayer, but so far always the answer has been the one that came to him: 'My grace is sufficient for thee' (2 Corinthians 12.9).

Any day that might change. What is *any* illness to Him? One touch and it would be gone. But I wonder if the Lord is saying not only to me but also to *you*, 'See to it that you are in perfect accord with Me and then trust Me to withhold no good thing.'

If health be that good thing, oh, how joyful it will be! Every morning I waken with the hope, 'Perhaps today'. But I want first to want His will, be that will mine or not. It is *there* that prayer can help most.

## Illness

I have only heard today of how very far from well you are.
I won't say what I feel about that. You are dearer to your
Lord than you are to me, and no good thing will He
withhold.

Life can be difficult. Sometimes the enemy comes like a
flood. But then is the time to prove our faith and live our
songs. A day or two ago when everything was feeling more
than usually impossible I opened on Psalm 40 with its new
song. 'He hath put a new song in my mouth, even praise.'
How like Him it is to 'put' it there. We couldn't find it for
ourselves, so He puts it. And when He puts it we can sing
it.

## Help comes

I have felt much with you during these days. Pain is never
easy to bear, and you have had so much of it. But help
comes, doesn't it? Strength for the day, strength for the
minute. And it will never fail us if only we look up.

Perhaps His word to you just now is the word He has
often spoken very tenderly to me: 'Let *Me* see thy
countenance, let *Me* hear thy voice' (Song of Songs 2.14).

## Written when a friend was in great pain

What a light from heaven your words brought! Your letter
came in a rather desperate hour, one of those hours when
the power of fear seems to be allowed to attack and weaken
one. Beside me stood N., saying over and over in agonizing
tones all that could be said about M.'s pain—and suddenly
I seemed to go right under. And then your letter came,
and as I read your verse it was as if the Lord spoke aloud:
'*These* are My words to you. He shall not be afraid of evil
tidings, his heart is fixed, trusting in the Lord.'

Those words swung me up out of that abyss of distress
and fear. And an hour later I heard that M. was out of
pain—asleep.

## Letters to one often ill

Life is a battle and always will be; we wouldn't wish it to be otherwise. But I don't like pain for you, or over-tiredness. I can only ask Him to fill your cup so full of joy that it will overflow *over* the tiredness, even as it did for Him when He sat by the well.

I am troubled about your sore throat and fever. I understand your perplexity. *Why* was Paul recaptured after being set free? Surely the Church had need of him? I often wonder so little is said of what must have been so terribly disappointing and perplexing.

But all our problems are open to Him and all will fit into His plan. *In the end* we shall see that what seems so hindering does not hinder but helps.

Now be at rest. This illness is not your doing. It is Satan's, and Satan can't chain the least of us without a word of permission from Him, and why He gives it we shall know one day. So let us claim again the blessing of the unoffended.

## Occupied in Thy statutes

Did you notice the words 'Occupied in Thy statutes' in
Psalm 119.23 Prayer Book Version? It is a beautiful word.
I have nothing to do today but to please Thee.

That is true of you, for this weariness is part of life,
bonds that are allowed to be. But I do hope for health and
ask for it. He knows what He is doing. 'Jesus Himself
knew what He would do.' There will be a lovely ending to
this story of frustration, something worth all it has cost.

## In His care

Trials are not 'chastisement'. No earthly father goes on
chastising a loving child. That is a common thought about
suffering, but I am quite sure it is a wrong thought. Paul's
sufferings were not that, nor are yours. They are battle
wounds. They are signs of high confidence—honours. The
Father holds His children very close to His heart when
they are going through such rough places as this.

'Thy *care* hath preserved my spirit'—a lovely Revised
Version Margin which helped me a few days ago—is my
word for you (Job 10.12). Think of it; all day long you are
being cared for, you are *in* His care.

## *A note to one who was ill*

You have had a long, long trial of faith. One comfort is, it is only a minute at a time and there is grace and patience given for each minute as it comes. I do trust the medicals will find the cause. There must be one.

I do understand (and so, and far more, does your Lord) the temptation to discouragement. Don't fear. It is only that the devil doesn't want you here at all. And in the end he is always beaten at that game.

# The way to God's Best

You don't need words to tell you how I am feeling about this weary pain. It seems sometimes that there is no way to God's Best but through pain, and yet how earnestly one longs to save a dear one from it.

Don't be disappointed about not being fit for work just yet. 'Let patience have her *perfect* work' has been one of the words set to me to learn by heart. I never found patience easy, being by nature a most impatient mortal; even one week in bed seemed impossible in old days. Well, I only tell you so to help you to know that I understand the ache to be well and up and out. And He understands far better than I do. I often think of those hours on the cross—helpless hours. He understands.

And the depression that follows pain He understands too. 'My soul cleaveth to the dust': no truer words were ever written. Sometimes just to know one is understood helps.

## *To one who had just had an operation*

I seemed to spend all night writing to you. The loving
Lord rest you now, and refresh and strengthen you. I shut
the doors of my mind when thoughts came about what the
days just after the operation must have been. I can't bear
to think of them. I have never had a major operation in my
life but have often nursed those who have had one, so I
know what these days can be. I shall not be easy till I hear
the next news.

These may be very tired days. It isn't easy to pick up
after such doings. But take the resting verses such as
Zephaniah 3.17 and John 15 ('Continue ye in My love',
*abide* there, like a child at home) and those psalms and
verses in the Gospels which show that side of life. 'Return
unto thy rest, O my soul.' 'Come unto Me and I will give
you rest.' 'My God shall supply all your need.' There are
hundreds such; take them as yours in a special way just
now, and don't tire your spirit and retard your recovery by
pressing against the limitations which for the present are
your fence of feathers. 'With His feathers has He made a
fence for thee' is a lovely rendering of Psalm 91.4. Nestle
under those feathers (He shall cover thee with His
feathers), and when you are tempted to press against the
fence, remember it is a fence of feathers—soft and downy,
and yet strong as the feathers of great birds are.

May those feathers be very comforting to you through
these days.

## To one whose father was ill

I have just come upon this jewel (in a most uncomfortable setting, but a jewel all the same): 'Know now that there shall fall unto the earth nothing of the word of the Lord' (2 Kings 10.10). I thought of one who is going through a bitter time—every possible arrow the archers can produce is being shot at that soul—and then I thought of you, and of your father and mother. Nothing of the word of the Lord spoken to you about your dearest shall fall unto the earth. Nothing they have ever known as His word to them shall fall.

Your brave mother will be marvellously strengthened, I believe, to help your father through this new trial of his faith. (How precious faith must be to the Lord.) He will be, I pray and believe for this, comforted by the God of all comfort.

Yes, I understand; how much easier it would be if one could bear pain for others—instead of them, I mean. I have often prayed that I might, for Colossians 1.24 RV seems to give ground for such a prayer, but never once has that joy been mine. So now I am learning to be content. Perhaps those of whom I am thinking specially would never have known Him as they know Him now if they had not suffered. Indeed it must be so. 'I never knew the comfort of God as I know it now', one said to me yesterday.

## Peace in Him

I have heard of your father's passing and can realize what this means to you.

As I thought of you I happened to see the words on the page of the Psalms which was open beside me. 'In the shadow of Thy wings will I make my refuge until these calamities be overpast.' They will not last for ever; it is always 'If for a season'. One day they will be overpast. And then verse 7 of Psalm 57 is yours too. 'My heart is fixed, O God, my heart is fixed. I will sing and give praise'—yes, however things are.

God bless you and guide you in all your ways. It is so good to be sure of your peace in Him.

## What an awakening!

I have felt alongside you through these days. What an awakening one who has walked with Him in the twilight must have, when suddenly she awakes in His likeness and the light is shining round her—all shadowy ways forgotten.

## Concerning a loved one's suffering

Don't forget when you imagine, all but see and hear and desperately feel, your loved one's pain, there is one thing that eludes you. That is the grace that is being given, the Presence that is there. But well I know how hard it is to carry on just as if all were going smoothly at home.

Yes, He often trusts us to trust Him when it does not seem as if He were providing. I have been through this rough stretch of road and so I can understand and walk it with you; and, best of all, He can, and He is nearer than near. Give your father my sheet anchor again, Job 34.29: 'When He giveth quietness, who then can make trouble?' It's such a victorious 'who'!

I think the Lord must find it difficult to teach us that here have we *no* continuing city. 'This is *not* your rest'; I often think of that. We know it, but we don't find it easy to live as if it were true. More and more I feel that we *are* what the Bible says we are—strangers and pilgrims. And all the things that happen are meant to emphasize that. But the pilgrim's God is very close to you and your father through these days.

## Fear not

This is for any of you who have those whom you love far away and in need of comfort.

A few nights ago I woke myself saying over and over again, Fear not. *Fear not.* One of those vivid dreams of friends in distress which somehow leave one in distress oneself was troubling me. A book usually distracts my mind when all else fails, but I couldn't read. So I asked Him who is 'about my bed' to let me have some good music. The wireless was by my bed, and I just touched the knob. Instantly the room filled with 'The Lord is my Shepherd, I shall not want'. The whole lovely Psalm was read in a full clear voice—and with it the benediction in Hebrews, 'Now the God of Peace that brought again from the dead our Lord Jesus, that great Shepherd of the sheep . . .'

I cannot tell you how wonderful it was and how close it brought Him, our Lord Himself. And I felt, if He can do this for one like me in so small a need, time so exactly the speaking of words six thousand miles away, cause the wireless to 'happen' to be tuned to catch them at that exact moment (2.15 a.m.), what can He not do for all His children everywhere?

Is there anything too kind for Him to do? No, there is *nothing* too kind for Him to do. So none of us needs fear for our dear ones. He who was so near to me then is as near to them, always.

## *Praise ye the Lord*

Last night a wonderful thing happened. I can't remember the last time it happened, it is so long ago. I slept practically all night and did not wake once in pain.

When I woke I could hardly believe it was morning, and I thought for a minute, 'Perhaps the bars are down and I am well!' I read Psalm 116, and everything in me was a song of hope and expectation. Then I found the bars were still there. But look at verse 19: 'In the courts of the Lord's House'—there are no iron bars, no suffering there—'praise ye the Lord'.

# 4  Tests and Trials

'Glorify ye the Lord
in the fires' (Isaiah 24.15),
not when they have passed
or you are out of them
and they are only memories,
but *in* them.

## Find harbour

I understand the buffetted days and the days of no small tempest, when neither sun nor stars appear. And it is good to pass through such days, for if we didn't we could neither prove our God nor help others. If any experience of ours helps to bring others to our Lord, what does any buffetting matter?

But we are not meant to live in a perpetual stormy sea. We are meant to pass through and find harbour and so be at peace. Then we are free from occupation with ourselves and our storms—free to help others.

I want to live in the light of the thought of His coming, His triumph—the end of this present darkness, the glory of His seen Presence. This bathes the present in radiance. You won't be sorry then that you trusted when you couldn't see, when neither sun nor stars in many days appeared and no small tempest lay on you (Acts 27.20). No, you won't be sorry then. So I won't be sorry now. I am believing. 'All joy and peace in believing': the words ring like a chime of bells.

## Dull days

Dry times are in a way trusted times. My word this morning was in Psalm 65.12, about the drops of His blessing falling on the pastures *of the wilderness*. It is a most comforting word.

Life, any life, can be stifled by the pettiness of the daily round. But yours won't be. One quick look up in the dullest moment and you are with Him whom your heart loves, your Life, your All.

All sorts of days come and go—they go, that's the best of them. Don't let the dull days pass without giving you what only dullness ever can give. It isn't the days of high tension that try us most, and so give us most; it's the days that seem all grey and dull. *They* test the quality of the gold. They prove it. 'Salute Apelles, the approved in Christ.' 'God knows, not we, the tests he stood' is Moule's note on Romans 16.10. I shall think of you as Apelles.

## Aloneness

I never noticed before the amazing way our Lord Jesus went through the trial of aloneness. I had thought of Him as surrounded by disciples after John 1.37–51, but I don't think it was so. I think He had them for a while and then sent them back to their ordinary work and *alone* went up to Jerusalem and *alone* was rejected at Nazareth. But He came through that trial of spirit unclouded. The people only saw 'a great light'. The Lord so bring us through whatever trial of spirit is appointed that at the end of the time there may be only a shining memory of a great light.

Isn't it lovely to see how every single trial that ever comes to us came to Him first? Hebrews 4.15 is a great word. He has been 'in all points' tempted just as we are.

This morning I feasted on a very familiar word, but it came freshly: John 17.20 RV, 'Neither for these only do I pray, but for them also that believe on Me through their word.' How much we value the prayers of one another; how dear they are to us. But His are dearer, far more precious. Oh, what manner of people we should be, prayed for by our Lord Himself!

# The way of the Cross

Don't be surprised if you are set at nought. It is part of the way of the Cross. Mark 9.12 says, 'The Son of Man must be set at nought.' If we follow in the way He went, we also must be set at nought. You will find this truer every year as you go on. And anything is easier. Scourging is easier. 'He must suffer many things, and' (as if this had to be mentioned very specially) *'be set at nought.'*

Have you ever gone through your New Testament marking the places where the iron of suffering in one form or another is mentioned? It's wonderfully enlightening. The book is full of joy I know, but it is also full of pain, and pain is taken for granted. 'Think it not strange. Count it all joy.'

We are meant to follow His steps, not avoid them. What if the suffering is caused by those whom we love? Was *His* not caused by those whom He loved? Oh, what a book the Bible is! If only we steep our souls in its mighty comfort we can't go far wrong—we shall never lose heart. 1 Peter 2.21: 'For hereunto were ye called: because Christ also suffered for you, leaving you an example, that ye should follow His steps.'

You will find the joy of the Lord comes as you go on in the way of the Cross. It was one who had nobody all his own on earth who said, 'If I am offered upon the sacrifice and service of your faith, I joy, and rejoice' (Philippians 2.17 RV). It is no small gift of His love, this opportunity to be offered upon the sacrifice and service; something you would not naturally choose, something that asks for more than you would naturally give. That's the proof of His love. So rejoice! You are giving Him what He asks you to give Him: the chance to show you what He can do.

## The only safe place

You are both, by His grace, counted worthy to follow the Crucified in the way of the Cross. So few are ready for that. They preach about it, sing about it, but when it comes to *doing it*, then they just don't. But I should not say 'they', 'I' is the pronoun. What do I know of this way? I shrank from it for you. *That* wasn't following.

What J. says is true, 'The Cross and the place of the fellowship of Christ's sufferings is the only safe place for those of us who have a responsibility for the souls of others.' Never will you regret the fellowship of sufferings.

I have been thinking today of our Lord's teaching in Mark 8.34 and kindred words. There is nothing offered on earth but a cross (and yet what joy is folded up in that offer!). 'He said unto all, If any man would come after Me, let him deny himself, and take up his cross daily and follow Me.' The Lord who did that Himself help us to do so too, not in word and prayer only but in deed—common deed. Isn't it comforting, sometimes, to know that His eye sees a cross in something that doesn't look like anything of the sort to others?

And after all, is there anything in all the world to be compared with the joy of doing His will? I know of no joy like it.

## Reviled, we bless

We are never likely to be under the curse that comes when all men speak well of us. In this case it is all so unexpected that we must keep low before our God and *not* wonder 'Why?' Faith never wonders why.

Just now the word I am saying over and over to myself is 'Being reviled, we bless'. That whole passage in 1 Corinthians 4 is speaking deep into me, for we are on the scrap-heap now, utterly and entirely, perhaps for the first time in our life. And I do think it is much easier to enjoy in prospect than in reality. 'Let my good name go hang, if only Christ be glorified.' Yes, that's it.

Aren't you glad that we need never stop loving? We may be disappointed, but love can go on. Only of course one can't depend in the old way. I think God lets such things happen partly that we may learn to discern. I find that difficult where I love, but one has to learn the lesson. Our dear Lord loved, but He did not commit Himself to all, for 'He knew what was in man'. Sometimes we, who do not know, do what He did not do and suffer for it.

There are times when spiritual discernment is the chief gift of the Spirit. The praised and made-much-of seldom have it. But those who have suffered the loss of all things, even their reputations—these, if they live with their Lord, have this gift.

## Led by His gentleness

I was wakened early this morning with you on my heart. All this that is asked of you is so much too much (from the human point of view) that I cannot forget it. Thank God, He doesn't either.

As I was praying I was led to Gideon's story, Judges 6.12–16. 'The Lord is with thee, thou mighty man of valour'—the last thing he felt himself to be. Then the question that comes if we allow it: 'If the Lord be with us, why then is all this befallen us? Where be all His miracles?' (*Why* is one person allowed to do such serious harm to His work?) 'And the Lord looked upon him, and said, Go in this thy might . . . Surely I am with thee.'

The 'why?' and the 'where?' are not answered. Perhaps they never will be answered on this side of eternity. But it was enough that He looked upon His son and was *surely* with him. So I will trust that the greatest of all miracles will be wrought once more. The humanly impossible will become the divinely possible, to the greater praise of His glory. The exceeding greatness of His power to you who believe will be made manifest.

But you will need a very quiet mind, a restful mind; so I will ask for this, as well as for strength of body, that you may go peacefully from one thing to the next—led by His gentleness.

# A Very Present Help

Which is harder, to do or to endure? I think to endure is much the harder, and our Father loves us too much to let us pass through life without learning to endure. So I want you to welcome the little difficult things, the tiny pricks and ruffles that are sure to come almost every day. For they give you a chance to say 'No' to yourself, and by doing so you will become strong not only to do but also to endure.

Whatever happens, don't be sorry for yourselves. You know how our Lord met the tempting 'Pity thyself' (Matthew 16.22 AV margin). After all, what is anything we have to bear in comparison with what our Lord bore for us?

I know that each one of you is in need of continual help if you are continually to conquer. I have splendid words to give you. They are from the first verse of Psalm 46—*a very present help.*

Our loving Lord is not just present, but nearer than thought can imagine, so near that a whisper can reach Him. You know the story of the man who had a quick temper and had not time to go away and pray for help. His habit was to send up a little telegraph prayer, 'Thy sweetness, Lord!', and sweetness came.

Do you need courage? 'Thy courage, Lord!' Patience? 'Thy patience, Lord!' Love? 'Thy love, Lord!' A quiet mind? 'Thy quietness, Lord!' Shall we all practise this swift and simple way of prayer more and more? If we do, our Very Present Help will not disappoint us. For Thou, Lord, hast never failed them that seek Thee.

# A cheerful giver

Don't offer grudgingly. That word came to me yesterday
with dreadful force, for it was just what I was doing
secretly in my heart. And the Lord does not love a
grudging giver but the other kind. '*Not* of necessity, for
God loveth a *cheerful* giver' (2 Corinthians 9.7 RV).

Believe me, this pain of yours will turn to a golden key.
Only keys of pure gold will open the innermost room of
hearts. I had a sorrow, and for years nothing happened
which in the least explained it. And then, I forget how
many years afterwards, a guest came here in dreadful
trouble. It was hidden under a bright, even gay manner,
and yet there it was. And if it had not been for the key that
my own grief gave me I could never have done anything for
her. *That* key opened the door. 'Not in vain in the Lord' is
written over suffering as well as over work.

## Accept with joy

I once wrote that God always answers us in the deeps, not in the shallows of our prayers. Hasn't it been so with you?

One of the hardest things in our secret prayer life is to accept with joy and not with grief the answers to our deepest prayers. At least I have found it so. It was a long time before I discovered that whatever came *was* the answer. I had expected something so different that I did not recognize it when it came.

And He doesn't explain. He trusts us not to be offended; that's all.

## The fellowship of His sufferings

The biggest wounds are wounds of the spirit, when the evil one seems to prevail and your heart is sore for some who will not turn to the Lord their Strength, but go on failing when they need not fail.

We share His grief then. I think we may feel glad that He isn't lonely over the souls who disappoint Him and us. We share in the fellowship of His sufferings over that soul. We share in the travail. But there is always 'more than an overweight of joy', especially in all work among precious little children.

## Disappointments

It takes all the sting out of a disappointment if we see it as
Paul did. Isn't it interesting that never once does he call
himself Nero's prisoner, though he was chained by Nero's
chain and in Nero's cell? This has been a great comfort to
me. We don't admit the domination of Nero—no, not for
an hour. We have to do only with the sovereignship of
Christ.

## The garden near the cross

How tangled life can be, and nobody can disentangle such tangles. Sometimes I wonder how I can spend one single moment on trifles, I should be all the time praying for those who are in tangles. But I do believe it is true that whatever I am doing, awake or asleep, the underlying thought is always there for those who are going through hard ways.

'Now in the place where He was crucified there was a garden.' It comforts me to know that you have found the garden—the garden that for ever lies so near the cross. And you will find it a place where the south wind blows as well as the north. It isn't all north wind.

But my chief word for you these days is the Song of Songs 8.5, 'Who is this that cometh up from the wilderness, leaning upon her Beloved?' I have just noticed afresh that He on whom we lean did Himself 'come out of the wilderness'. He doesn't ask us to walk in any path where He has not walked before.

Now may His joy be yours. As that beautiful book, *Religio Medici*, has it, 'Dispose of me according to the wisdom of Thy pleasure. Thy will be done through my own undoing.' In what different ways, but how truly, those words fit you and me. I shall feast on this book today. But oh, to *live* it!

## *Even the death of the cross*

To each of us there is something which seems simply impossible to get on top of. I know my special foe and all this week I have had to live looking off to Jesus, the Author and (thank God) the Finisher of our faith. (I have just now turned to Hebrews 12.2 to make sure that word is really there.) Psalm 138.8 is another standby. Oh! blessed be the eternal word of God. Feelings may change (they do), we may change and fall (we do), but His word stands steadfast. It *cannot* fail.

Don't you think that some of us *must* know the trials of misty weather if we are to be enabled to understand when others are in the mist?

My word yesterday was '*Even* the death of the cross'. There is an 'even' in most lives. God help us not to shrink back from that 'even' (Philippians 2.8).

## To one in trouble

I want to give you a word that helped me all yesterday and will help me today. It is the 'through' of Psalm 84.6 and of Isaiah 43.2, taken with Song of Songs 8.5.*

We are never *staying* in the valley or the rough waters; we are always only passing through them, just as the bride in the Song of Songs is seen coming up from the wilderness leaning upon her Beloved.

So whatever the valley is, or however rough the waters are, we won't fear. Leaning upon our Beloved we shall come up from the wilderness and, as Psalm 84.6 says, even use the valley as a well, *make* it a well. We shall find the living waters there and drink of them.

---

* *Psalm 84.6*: Passing through the valley of Weeping they make it a place of springs (A.V.—make it a well).

*Isaiah 43.2*: When thou passest through the waters, I will be with thee; and through the rivers, they shall not overflow thee.

*Song of Songs 8.5*: Who is this that cometh up from the wilderness, leaning upon her beloved?

# Silence

You are sitting on the well-side with your Lord who once was weary and sat thus on the well. You don't see Him, but He is there. You are His honoured one: 'Blessed are they that have not seen and yet have believed.'

The bog myrtle you gave me is in my *Daily Light*, and every day its sweetness is a special little joy to me. It knows nothing of that. It only knows it is dried up, a withered thing. I wonder if in its freshest days it was sweeter than it is now.

Times of dryness are times when we are meant to live in the middle line of Zephaniah 3.17 RV margin: 'He will rejoice over thee with joy, He will be silent in His love, He will joy over thee with singing.' Our dear Lord does not misunderstand silence. Offer Him your silence and accept His, 'I will be silent in My love.' Songs are not far away. They are on either side of the Silence. It is folded up in song.

Now be at rest. He is not looking at you with *dis*-pleased eyes. Oh no, I can all but see just the opposite.

## Trusted

How you are trusted, and you will not disappoint Him who is trusting you. I suppose one of His greatest trusts is a big disappointment. This is that. So we will look up and praise Him and sing to Him. 'What a God who *out of shade* nest for singing bird hath made.' Any bird will sing in the sunlight, but there are some who sing in the shade; bulbuls do. I have often heard them in the dullest, rainiest weather. You are God's bulbul.

You are right not to write details about the pricking thorns of life. It only makes them prick more sharply. Look at the roses on your brier, and as you think of them your heart will lighten. I used to thank Him, when my skies were a bit cloudy, that there was so much more blue than grey. I know the same is true of your skies, in spite of these horrid injections and other things.

I understand about your dread of pain. And *He* understands, He who bore pain unimaginable and unforgettable. Our scars won't be eternal. His are.

## For Easter

'Now in the place where He was crucified there was a garden' (John 19.41). This is my Easter word for you. You will find your garden very near to the place where you will be crucified.

'Always bearing about in the body the dying of the Lord Jesus *that the life also of Jesus might be made manifest in our body*' (2 Corinthians 4.10). Whenever we have been most earnest and most sensitive about bearing about in our body that dying, we have known most of the power and sweetness and unearthly joy of the life of our Lord.

## Easter Day

This is a wonderful day. The more we think of it, the more wonderful it is. But somehow I keep going back to what led up to this day of joy. The true triumph of love was not on Easter morning; it was won on the cross when the Lord said, *It is finished*.

The choir sang 'The suffering night is over' to me. Ever since, the lines

> Forgive me, Lord, if I
> My small griefs magnify

have been in my heart. I do pray that I may not magnify my small griefs. Don't magnify yours. They will be so soon over, it is not worth while. Also if we do so, they lose their power to perfect us. When we accept them as His good, lovable and perfect will, then, I believe, they work together to make us more usable to our beloved Lord. And isn't that all that matters?

Bodies are curious things. My favourite word came in my reading today. 'As we have borne . . . we shall also bear' (1 Corinthians 15.49). We certainly have borne the image of the earthly; there isn't any doubt about that. And as certain as that is, so certain is the wonderful truth whose meaning we cannot fully understand: *we shall also* bear the image of the heavenly.

That's something to look forward to!

# The cup

You know how the four Gospels tell the story of
Gethsemane. Each is a little different, but all are true.
They fit into one another and make a picture that, if you
ever have to suffer, will mean everything to you. I will take
words from only two Gospels. In St Mark we read that our
Lord said, 'Abba, Father, all things are possible unto
Thee; *take away this cup from Me*: nevertheless not what I
will, but what Thou wilt' (Mark 14.36). And in St John we
read that He said, '*The cup which My Father has given Me,
shall I not drink it?*' (John 18.11).

You will have no peace until you pass from those first
words to the second. But this may not come in a day. Be
patient. He who prayed in an agony that the cup might be
removed will be patient with you, for He understands just
what you are feeling. Yet He will not rest until He brings
you to the place where He stood when He said, 'The cup
which My Father has given Me, shall I not drink it?'

I find much comfort in Psalm 138.3, 'In the day when I
cried Thou answeredst me, and strengthenedst me with
strength in my soul.' 'In the day that I cried': that does not
mean the day after, or an hour or two, or even a minute
after, but *that very day, that very hour, that very minute.* God
hears us the moment we cry and strengthens us with the
only kind of strength that is of any use at all.

# 5 Joy and Satisfaction

There is joy, joy found nowhere else,
when we can look up into Christ's face
when He says to us,
'Am I not enough for thee, Mine own?'
with a true, '*Yes, Lord, Thou art enough*'.

# Unshadowed joy

May this year be one of unshadowed joy. There need never be a shadow. All shadows are from beneath, from self, from the *I* in us which so often wants us to listen to what it says, instead of to the voice of our Lord. Let us refuse this self voice, always, and live in the unclouded light of selfless joy and love. This is what I want to do ever more and more.

I have a lovely word for you: Luke 4.30. 'Jesus passing through the midst of them went His way.' We are meant to pass through the midst of whatever comes and not get upset or even inwardly ruffled.

A day or two ago I was thinking rather sadly of the past—so many sins and failures and lapses of every kind. I was reading Isaiah 43, and in verse 24 I saw myself: 'Thou hast wearied Me with thine iniquities.' And then for the first time I noticed that there is no space between v.24 and v.25, 'I, even I, am He that blotteth out thy transgressions for Mine own sake; and I will not remember thy sins.' Who but our Father would forgive like that?

## *Joy is eternal*

I was thinking partly of my own need and partly of you
when I opened my Bible at Luke 24.26. 'Ought not Christ
to have suffered these things, and to enter into His glory?'
It was the 'ought not' that laid hold on me. I must not wish
less than He accepted as something that 'ought' to be, for
any of you. It is easier far to accept for oneself than for
another. And yet the Father and the Blessed Spirit, and
the loving angels too, accepted it for the holy Son of God.

I am glad that the 'Enter into the joy of thy Lord' is the
certain ending of everything that is so painful today for
you who travail to save the souls for whom Christ died.
And all that travail means is only for a moment. 'If for a
season . . .' 'After that ye have suffered awhile . . .' Joy,
not suffering, is eternal.

And there are many joys now. May your day be full of
joy, the kind that is strength.

# The jewel of His joy

As I think of you I can only commit you to the One who loves you best. You know perhaps, Lilias Trotter's painting of a whin blossom (gorse, you call it); beside it she wrote, 'Setteth in pain the jewel of His joy'. I think of you like that.

I am very sure that the jewel of His joy is for you, prepared, held safe for you. But I see it 'set' in pain, and I could not bear it for you if it were not for another word—the word 'choose' in Psalm 47.4. 'Choose after testing', as David chose the best five pebbles for his purpose in the brook; choose after testing all other choices. And He who chooses is above all circumstances, has the choice of all. So when He chooses the inheritance of a beloved one, it *must* be 'the excellency of Jacob', the best He could possibly choose, the excellency of Jacob whom He loved.

I cannot forget the flints on my own path and the thorns. But, looking back, I know I would not have chosen any other if I could have known when first I began to walk in it what it would mean of His companionship, and also of the power to enter into the griefs of others. It was all worth while, ten thousand times worth while.

Don't let anything discourage you. Some may disappoint you—He was disappointed. You will find that nothing is too small for His regard. He will say things to you that you could not repeat—they would sound too small, too intimate—but they will be the joy and rejoicing of your heart.

## Receiving and reflecting

It has been a wonderful year and the next will be more wonderful, for the path does not grow duller as we go on but brighter—it shineth more and more unto the perfect day. And light is sown on that path, and gladness.

I think of you as continually 'receiving and reflecting', as Rotherham translates 2 Corinthians 3.18. 'And we all with unveiled face receiving and reflecting the glory of the Lord into the same image are being transformed, from glory into glory.'

The Lord Jesus keep you so and increase your clearness of vision that the reflection may be the more perfect. And pray this prayer for me. I do feel such a dull mirror, and I need your prayers.

## The joy of the Holy Spirit

Yes, peace is the gift of gifts. This morning I read the two letters to the Thessalonians. Don't you think it is lovely that 'the joy of the Holy Spirit' should be mentioned in connection with suffering? I think it is the only place where the Spirit's joy is mentioned; you might check this, but I think it is true. You are now in a very good position to prove that gift of joy. It is easy to rejoice when everything is as one wishes it were. But when things are exactly as one wishes they were not, it is not so easy. Then is the time to prove the things we believe.

Your whole life now is a proving of His power to enable you to do *anything*. You will never be able to fear again, I think, after all this.

## He will satisfy

He will be enough for you. 'Shall never thirst' is a true word, and whatever His thoughts may be for your life, He will satisfy you. '*Thou*, O Lord, art the thing that I long for.' And to you He says, 'I have longed for thee.' That deep wonderful word amazes me again and again. Psalm 132.14 Prayer Book Version: 'For the Lord hath chosen Zion to be a habitation for Himself: He hath longed for her.'

And now to Him who heard 'what time the storm fell upon thee', to the tenderest of tender ones who can quiet our restless longings and teach us to do without, till our soul is even as a weaned child—to Him whose you are I commit you.

## Count them happy

Yesterday the two blue love-birds were in my room. They were flying about happily when Marahatha the barbet, whose tail is very short, evidently thinking their tails much too long, with one tweak tweaked out the long blue feathers. That love-bird looked very sorry for himself, and I was very sorry for him. So was everybody. I think we often think of those whose hopes are suddenly ended much as we all looked at the poor love-bird as he hopped about (you know the funny strut of a love-bird) inviting sympathy. We say, 'poor thing'. What low levels content us. God forgive us for our grovelling. They are happy—we must count them happy—that endure. James was right (James 5.11).

# Rejoice!

This morning Psalm 70.4 spoke to me. 'Let all those that seek Thee rejoice and be glad in Thee.' That's not just a holy aspiration, it's a command. And He who commands enables. Let all those who seek the Lord *rejoice*, today, every day. Joy is to be the keynote of our lives. He calls us then to make an act of faith every time we would naturally be pulled down into the pit of joylessness, for there is an end set to the sin and sorrow and confusion of the world as well as to our own private trials. We only see today. He whom we worship sees tomorrow.

You will find the truest joy comes in utter self-forgetfulness—what our Lord called the *denial* of self. This is what He is working in you to create and maintain. But He never forgets the cost.

Now may God give you the joy of Psalm 4.7, 'Thou hast put gladness in my heart, more than they have when their corn and their wine are increased.' May that joy flow over and wash away self in all its subtle forms and give you that dearest of all graces, *selflessness*.

## Joy

Don't let your mind dwell on sadness as it saps the soul of strength. There is more blue sky overhead than clouds. The clouds will pass. I often think how sad we shall be at the end, if we have failed in joy. I don't want to fail.

## The happy-hearted

He has brought you into the company of the happy-hearted, and you will carry His happiness wherever you go. How we dishonour our good Master when we carry fogs and mists and a general sense of dreariness. The Lord of Joy keep us in the glorious way of joy.

## Joys are on their way

Joys are always on their way to us. They are always travelling to us through the darkness of the night. There is never a night when they are not coming (Psalm 30.5).

## Fullness of joy

Truly He does give happiness. I'm never unhappy except when I hear of wrongdoing or think of the grief of the world. It's strange how one can be happy when underneath all the time there is the thought of His grief. And yet it is true that there is happiness, for continually He is doing such loving things that it would be quite impossible not to know that He is here. And if He is here, 'about my bed' as Psalm 139.2 says, how could there be anything but fullness of joy? 'In Thy Presence is fullness of joy', not only hereafter but now.

I think of you going to school now in fullness of joy, teaching, influencing, loving in fullness of joy, for you are in His presence, never out of that blessedness for one minute. We should be the most radiant of people with such a Lord.

## In His footsteps

Just now I am reading through the Gospels and marking in the margin every place where suffering is mentioned. It is mentioned very often. The Lord Jesus made it plain from the beginning that there would be trial of many kinds for all who would follow Him, and He Himself led the way in that path. Should we be surprised when we find ourselves following in His footsteps?

There is joy too. He said clearly that sorrow would be turned into joy, joy that would never end. But I think that He wants us all to understand quite definitely that if we follow in the way of the cross we must be prepared to take up the cross. We must not think of life as a joy-ride. But there is nothing whatever to be afraid of. 'Blessed are they that dwell in Thy house: they will be always praising Thee' is a shining word for us all.

No one knows what this next year will bring, but one thing is sure. He will be with us, and He is enough for every difficulty that may arise. He is enough for today's difficulty. Do you sometimes feel like the disciples when they were in the midst of the sea toiling in rowing, for the wind was contrary to them? Then take the lovely words for your comfort: 'He cometh unto them and saith unto them, Be of good cheer: it is I; *be not afraid.*'

No matter how much the wind blows, it will be true for us as it was for them, 'The wind ceased'. So let us be of good cheer and go on our way rejoicing.

# Letters to her children

## (1) Stars

You have given me a starry joy. When I gave you your name (Star) I prayed that you might grow up to be a star in this dark world, and now you are learning some of the wonder of the stars. Do you know that Venus is always covered with cloud and mist, and that it is the light shining on the mist which makes it look so beautiful? Isn't this a figure of the true?

Sometimes what feels like a cloud and mist is allowed to come and seems to cover us. But it doesn't matter. If only the sun of the love of the Lord shines upon us, the very mist and cloud will be turned to beauty.

Isn't it wonderful to think that all the Bible people and our Lord Himself looked at those very same stars and constellations? The first time I realized that, I gazed and gazed at the shining worlds.

And another wonderful thing is that the stars are shining all day long, passing over our heads by day as by night—only we can't see them till it is dark. There is a lovely meaning in that, but I leave you to find it out for yourself.

I am very glad you shared the joy of stars with me. Now I share it with you.

# Letters to her children

## (2) All that I have is thine

I am very, very glad when I think of you, because your whole life is given to your Saviour and I know that one day He will say to you, 'Enter into the joy of thy Lord'.

He does satisfy the heart of His loving, trusting child. You have found Him true, I know, just as I have, and tens of thousands have. No one who gave herself wholly to Him was ever disappointed at the end. No, not one.

And all the time He is with you, my child. He says to you, 'Daughter, thou art ever with Me and all that I have is thine.' He notices everything, remembers everything, gives everything His dear child needs for life and service. She is ever with Him, never, never far away from His loving heart.

If this note is ever in your hands it will be because I am out of sight, with the Lord. But I shall not be forgetting you. I do not forget you now although I see you so seldom. I shall be thinking of you, loving you, praying for you, rejoicing as I see you run your race.*

God bless you and make you a blessing.

---

* On another occasion, Amy wrote: 'Surely being with Him will mean a new power to pray? It must, I think, for to be present with the Lord must mean access in a far more vital sense than is possible now, and surely that will mean a new power to speak to Him about our beloved?'

# 6 Love and Trust

More and more I feel that love
is the golden secret of life.
The very air of heaven is love,
for God is love and love never fails.
So go on loving not only the loveless
but the unlovable, the difficult,
the perplexing, the disappointing—
unto the end.

## Loving adoration

All round us is the great, dark, unloving world. How very few care for our Saviour; even those who are called by His name sometimes offer Him a very cold kind of affection. He said on the cross, *I thirst*, and even now His love is athirst for love.

Form the habit of using everything that speaks of His presence to remind you of Him, and as you are so reminded, lift up your heart in loving adoration. 'Lord, I love Thee; I who am dust of Thy dust, I love Thee; I worship Thee; I adore Thee.'

If only you do this, then of one thing I am sure. You will not only love one another so tenderly that unkindness will be impossible, but every man, woman and child who comes to you will feel some touch of His kindness. Love will flow round everyone and far beyond—who can tell how far? And best of all, there will be refreshment for Him as of a drink of cool water on a hot day.

## *Trust God's love*

I have been thinking of 1 John 4.16, which in one translation says, 'We have come to understand and to trust the love which God hath in us.' We can never fully understand that love, but we can begin to understand it even here and now, and as we understand we trust. This means that we trust all that the love of God does; all He gives and does not give, all He says and all He does not say. To it all we say, by His most loving enabling, *I trust*.

Here is a little song; it is my gift to you all.

> Father of spirits, this my sovereign plea
> I bring again and yet again to Thee.
>
> Fulfil me now with love, that I may know
> A daily inflow, daily overflow.
>
> For love, for love, my Lord was crucified,
> With cords of love He bound me to His side.
>
> Pour through me now; I yield myself to Thee,
> O Love that led my Lord to Calvary.

## Double my love

As I think of you I think of words written by one who warred and suffered about six hundred years ago, Raymond Lull. 'Say, O Lover,' asked the Beloved, 'if I double thy trials, wilt thou still be patient?' 'Yea,' answered the Lover, 'so that Thou double also my love.' I am quite sure that the Beloved will double the love of His Lover, if at any time He doubles the trials.

I think also of those words in Hebrews that go to the depths of all suffering and 'speak to our condition' when no others seem to touch us: Hebrews 2.10, 'For it became Him . . . in bringing many sons unto glory to make the Captain of their salvation perfect through suffering.' I am writing on the day after you knew that this joy of joys had been given to you—the joy, I mean, of bringing a dear child into the way of glory.

I give you Hebrews 10.35, 36 for the worst days that will ever come. 'Cast not away therefore your confidence, which hath great recompense of reward. For ye have need of patience, that, having done the will of God, ye may receive the promise.' I commit you to Him who bequeathed His peace to us just before He faced His cross. I commit you to Him who is your best beloved. He will never leave thee nor forsake thee; the work of righteousness (which is obedience) shall be peace, and the effect of righteousness quietness and assurance for ever.

## Dictated, for her family

I don't find it easy to be without writing to you. One morning I found myself saying, 'Lord, it is very hard to be silent when one loves.' Then suddenly I remembered the words we know so well, Zephaniah 3.17 RV margin, 'He will be silent in His love'. Love in silence is often the deepest love of all.

Another thought has brought comfort to me. Sometimes things are allowed to happen so that the quiet power of our Lord to arrange and rearrange events according to His purpose may be shown. The priests did not want Him to be arrested before the feast was over, but He had planned otherwise. 'After two days', He said to His disciples, 'the Passover cometh and the Son of Man is delivered to be crucified.' And so it was. He, not the Priests, decided the order of events. Even so, all through the confusions of life, the quiet purpose of the Lord is fulfilled and nothing can upset it.

It is a splendidly reassuring truth for us, who do truly want His way. There is quietness and assurance in the calmness of our Lord. Although things have been difficult for some of you, His peaceful purpose has been carried out.

Not being able to write has meant much more time spent with God for you, each one separately. It is as if I were with you far more truly than in the flesh, and there has sometimes been a power given to hold you and all your needs steadily in the presence of the Lord. It is good that we have such an understanding God. This little note only tells you what you know, that I am with you in spirit, loving you all more than ever, if that can be.

## Free to love

A few minutes ago I read words that sum up my desires for you: 1 Thessalonians 3.12, 'The Lord make you to increase and abound in love one toward another, and toward all men, even as we also do toward you.' I do indeed know that increasing and abounding love, but the words 'toward all men' I want specially to be true of you.

This poor world is a cold place to many. I pray that no one who comes to us may ever feel chilled here, but rather that all chilliness may melt, melted by the blessed glow of heavenly love made manifest. Don't let us ever be afraid of being too loving. We can never love enough.

So I pray, 'Lord, keep all my children free to love. Never let the slightest shade of suspicion shadow any heart. Help each to think the best of every other. Through all the chances and changes of life, hold all together in tender love. Let nothing quench love. Let nothing cool it. Keep every thread of the gold cord unbroken, unweakened, even unto the end. O my Lord, Thou Loving One, keep my beloveds close together in Thy love for ever.'

## The canary

I have a canary all by himself in a big cage in my room.
His name is Cymbal because he sings beautifully. *But he
can't get on with other canaries.* That is why he is alone in
my room. He doesn't like to sing with them, or eat with
them, or play with them.

Is there anyone with whom you don't get on? With
whom you don't like to work, or play, or do anything?
Perhaps you haven't actually quarrelled, but if you can
avoid it if you don't talk together, and you don't care to pray
together.

If there be such a one, will you do this? Every day will
you name that one to your Lord? (Don't mention faults,
but just ask for a blessing.) I do earnestly ask you to do
this. Will you do it?

## The heavenly river

Yes, the wings of anxious thought must be let down if we are to hear His peaceful words. I have been reading some of them this morning in Romans 8. Those blessed words about love remind me of what you say. We need never, never fear that the stream of love will run dry. The heavenly river, the river of God which is full of water, never will. And so, as drop by drop we seem to be drained dry, it is only seeming. It isn't really so. It cannot be so. For more love is perpetually pouring through us, 'love instead of love'.

Your friend will find it so. All will seem to be used up, all strength, all that she has to give, and then more will come. She will reign in life—another of the words in Romans that are fathomless.

But I know well that these are hard days. His were hard. We don't want ease when He had rough ways. She is tired for His name's sake. Jesus being weary sat there on the well. How glad we shall be afterwards that we were allowed to be weary for Him.

Yes, love is a glorious thing, new every morning. There is nothing to fear if there is love. 'Lord, do Thou turn me all into love, and all my love into obedience. And let my obedience be without interruption.' (Saint Augustine)

## *God wants lovers*

You will, I believe and trust, become more and more in love with a crucified Saviour. He wants lovers. Oh how tepid is the love of so many who call themselves by His name. How tepid our own—my own—in comparison with the lava fires of His eternal love. I pray that you may be an ardent lover, the kind of lover who sets others on fire.

## For a birthday

The Lord bless you. Everything I want to say is in that prayer. I have been reading St John. 'He that loveth Me shall be loved of My Father, and I will love him and will manifest Myself to him.'

So I ask for this mighty thing for you, the 'conscious experience of love' (Westcott), the clearness of His all-but-seen presence, something far, far more than we are usually satisfied with. We are only at the edge of the sea; oh, to swim out into the sunrise!

Now may that satisfying love enfold you.

## *Our most precious possession*

I want to ask you to be very careful about love; it is our
most precious possession. Don't let it be weakened
anywhere. Be loving. Be courteous to one another. I have
known some who thought that if one loved one could be
rude. Love is never rude. Look not on your own things but
on the things of others. What can you do today to make
someone happy? *Do that.*

Now God bless you all. I shall be loving you to the
end—and there is no end to love.

## God gives love

God gives love; it isn't in us to love. I don't naturally love people I don't know (and I don't naturally love all the people I do know!). Love is of God and from God, and He pours it into our hearts if we let Him.

Our Lord did not say, 'Go ye into all the world if you feel an ardent flame of love to all the people in it.' He just said, 'Go ye', and as we obey He gives us all we need to lead them to Him. And of course as we most of all need love, He gives it to us.

So fear not. God hath given us a spirit not of fear, but of power and of love and of discipline.

## To one in need

Are you getting plenty of quiet with God? Remember the words I so often quote from Jeanne De Chantal. 'We cannot measure the love He showers on souls who give and abandon themselves to Him, and who have no higher aspiration than to do all that they believe to be pleasing to Him.' If only we live so, then there can be nothing to fear; we shall radiate peace and joy and love, and the shout of a King will be ever among us.

You often remind me of myself. Too much of your nature is exposed to the winds that blow upon it. You and I both need to withdraw more and more into the secret place with God. Do you know what I mean, I wonder?

# Trust Jesus

Operations have been going on gaily here, and on Monday some boys had tonsils and adenoids done. Among them was N., a nervous little fellow. Just before he went to the theatre he said to one of the others (recalling an illustration given in a children's service a fortnight before): 'When I lie down on the table I will do this' (and he touched the fingers on one hand, spelling T-R-U-S-T, and then he touched the fingers on his other hand, spelling J-E-S-U-S) 'and I will clasp my hands, and I will wake up smiling.'

They tell me this is exactly what he did. He clasped his hands, went to sleep most peacefully and woke up as he said he would, smiling. Rather nice, wasn't it? These operations have been a great test of character, and the thing is to smile the first minute one can. But to 'wake up smiling' was a new idea.

## *To one caring for boys*

After baptism when Satan attacks, it is easy for a boy to become discouraged, and you also will be tempted to be discouraged. But go on hoping. Again and again when I had all but lost hope I used to go to the God of Hope and ask for the gift of hope. Never be shaken in hope. Never be cooled in love. Never get tired of loving and hoping—yes, and believing.

Our Lord has long patience. We too must have long patience, for souls can't be hurried. He whom we follow, having loved His own, loved them unto the end. May His love fill us, strengthen us, be in us hope and faith and patience—yes, and joyful expectation. We shall reap—*you* will reap—if we faint not.

One can't help anyone whom one doesn't love enough to bear with, even as our angels bear with us. We must be most trying to them at times.

# Tranquil faith

'Great peace have they which love Thy law: and nothing shall offend them' (Psalm 119.165). Yesterday I had a new little lesson in this. I couldn't think or do anything, and hardly realizing what I was about I kept on repeating inside, over and over, 'Why can't I think? Why can't I do?' At last I opened Kay, which was on my book-rest, and the book opened at Psalm 37.7, 'Be silent to the Lord, and wait patiently for Him.' Be silent. Don't ask questions. O rest in the Lord, wait patiently for Him. 'The silence is that of tranquil faith' is Kay's note.

So I shall ask for you tranquil faith, radiant peace. 'They looked unto Him and were radiant.' *That* radiance does not depend upon circumstances.

## Amy's last word

*As Amy's life drew to a close, writing of any kind became impossible. Her last letter, undated, was written in pencil in large, sprawling letters which straggled across the page:*

## Precious Child

If so dear to me, what to Him?

*Amma*